# Sukulu Ĩte Ngũta

## The School With No Walls

### *Where Lifelong Lessons Begin*

"*The School With No Walls* is a wonderful and warm expression of learning and of continuous lessons of growth presented in a way that all may benefit. Vincent Kituku has a unique perspective...his messages are humble, yet wise and universal. They provide a standard by which values can be defined and applied in our lives. His stories allow us to appreciate that which would otherwise go unnoticed in our lives; particularly as we struggle with day-to-day issues." *Larry Crowley, President, Idaho Power Resources Corporation; Boise, Idaho.*

"As with 'things we learned in kindergarten' so many of life's lessons become more vivid and meaningful when presented as a story or fable. In addition, Kituku's collection in *The School With No Walls* teaches us that the important concepts for successful living are universal, transcending time and cultures. An excellent read for any age." *Hal Rumsey, President, Premier Financial Group; Boise, Idaho.*

"The School With No Walls is a reminder of the never ending truth: Common sense prevails." *Glen Smith, Retired Award-winning Salesman for Sears; Elyria, Ohio.*

"Dr. Kituku's anthology of quotes and insights from his native culture are both inspiring and delightful to read. A real treasure for my whole family to enjoy." *Clay Conner, President, Wellness Technologies; Boise, Idaho.*

"Learning about life, and our individual role in it, does occur outside the formal classroom setting. While I grew up in a different region of the world than Dr. Kituku, I still remember my Grandfather's teachings and words of wisdom regarding my 'piece of the national cake.' As I read and reflected on the lessons contained in the book, my mind could not help returning again and again to my grandfather, the solitude and comfort of his workshop and his views of life's mysteries and challenges. We all have those individuals of influence in our lives and not only should we listen carefully, but we should prepare ourselves to pass it forward. As such, this book gently reminds me of my obligation to my own children." *Dennis Dreher, Director, International Student Services; University of Wyoming.*

"... Classic education does an adequate job of teaching facts and abstracts. The educators are dedicated, hardworking, and often times inspiring people. But the 'classroom' education doesn't always teach life skills necessary today. Grandmothers and grandfathers, aunts and uncles, the extended family with accumulated wisdom, and the village itself can provide the safety net to allow children the courage and security to try... I hope that those of you who hear and read Dr. Kituku's words will be motivated enough to learn in *The School With No Walls.* Join me in a fun and knowledge filled class." *Ted Gibson, Auto Parts Manager, Bob Rice Dealership; Boise, Idaho.*

# Sukulu Ĩte Ngũta

## The School With No Walls
### *Where Lifelong Lessons Begin*

By

**Dr. Vincent Mũli wa Kĩtukũ**

Library of Congress Number 97-92977

ISBN 0-9650780-7-8


Forward: Dr. Rex Ellis

Illustrations: Susan Ballenger

Cover Illustration: Kelly Matthews

Layout and Cover Design: Brian Jackson


Printed in the United States of America

First Printing: 1997

# *Dedication*

To my beloved children who are also my teachers. Somebody once said, "Every adult needs to teach a child. That is how adults learn." I have learned above and beyond my expectations from you all.

**Kasiva** (Kasiva is my mother's name and now it has been passed on to my first born).

**Mbinya** (my mother-in-law's name that has been passed on to my second child).

**Ndinda**, my third child (implying "long stay").

**Kithetheesyo**, my fourth child and first son (meaning persistence).

Also to the preservation of the Kamba community heritage which is a tremendous source of pride and inspiration.

# Table of Contents

# *Acknowledgments*

Thanks to Kasiva, my mother, for being the brain of this book. On July 23, 1996 from midnight till 4:00 a.m., she listened as I recited positive statements she or dad said to us when we were growing that have had profound influence in our lives. Both of my parents taught that each individual comes to this world with special talents and a mission. Sometimes, however, others have to present an individual with something to live up to, for that individual to achieve his/her potential and accomplish his/her mission on earth. My parents are natural teachers, teaching in the *School With No Walls*. Tata na Mama, ngai amuathime (Dad and Mom, God bless you).

Thanks to my wife, friend and life partner, Wanza wa Muli for her love, support, great cooking, traditional and modern academic input towards this undertaking. May God bless you in a special way!! To Prof. Stan Steiner, a book lover, and his beloved wife, Joy Steiner, a professional storyteller, for your desire to have the Boise community exposed to the rich world cultures. To Brian and Donna Jackson for your creative input and encouragement. Many have edited or made comments about this book. Mūtūnga Thyaka (my brother-in law) edited the Kikamba text, Ted

i

Gibson, Tara Dunow, Mary Graesch, Nancy Macintosh and others edited the English text. Thank you all.

Special thanks to members of service clubs in the Treasure Valley area. For six months, I visited most of your clubs and learned that all cultures have the same hopes, concerns and fears. You are laying the foundation for all of us to spring forth and seize our future with hope as we experience our own *School With No Walls*. All students and workshop attendees who have participated in my presentations showed me one lesson: that you love someone because you know their story. Tell stories.

# *Foreword*

"Give anyone something to live up to (not down to) and the skies won't be their limit." What a wonderful way to say, believe in yourself and you can achieve far more than you can imagine.

This and many other wonderful lessons from the *School With No Walls* is available for you to enjoy in this collection by Dr. Vincent M. Kituku. Sometimes we don't need a sermon, a lecture or a speech to remind us of what we already know and have lost sight of, or what we know to be true, but can't find a way to express simply.

Well here you are. Here, in a fine collection that hails from East Africa but easily translates to other cultures, is a collection of reminders that there is more to learn from the experiences of our collective lives, than there is in any one textbook—no matter how comprehensive.

My daddy calls it "mother wit." He also calls it "simple common sense." It was neither for me. It was only "simple" for those who understood the message. For those of us who did not, it took a bit more time to realize that "simplicity has a complicated beginning." So Vincent has taken his work a little further. He has explained his proverbs in ways that elaborate on their meaning.

This is not a difficult book to understand. In fact, as you read it, you may feel that it is worth only one reading since a great deal of what is being said, "makes sense." I would advise you to read it again ... and again ... and again. You will find that as you travel through the various stages of your life, the words and their meaning will grow richer. You will find that the words grow with you, and that as you mature, the universal themes and reminders they contain will be like old friends. They will keep you on the path that is best for you.

There is a story on every page. Not only the story Vincent remembers, that calls up the verses he offers us, but the stories in your life that affirm for you that these proverbs connect with your life, your experiences, and your culture.

As you read these jewels, move them beyond East Africa and into your particular experience. And if they motivate you to remember, treasure and most importantly, pass on your own stories ... I think Vincent will smile.

**Dr. Rex M. Ellis**
**Smithsonian Institute**
**Museum Studies**

# *From the Author*

My grandfather, Musoo wa Nzavi, told me over and over that, "The great and life-lasting school has no walls." Now, 30 years later, I can affirm he was right.

The school he talked about is not where we learn to be an economist, conservationist, mechanic, or any other career. It is where we learn the connectivity of life. Who Am I? Who is my God? Who is next to me? What is surrounding us? What is the essence of living? What are the values that make life liveable? What can we learn from both wild and cultivated plants? Are there lessons from animals, both domesticated and undomesticated which can enrich our lives? What is the value of hope? What is a better investment than the investment in one's trust, hope, talents, gifts, experiences, fears, love for his family, co-workers and the community? What amount of strength should one use to hold to those material possessions which can be gained, lost and regained? How much energy on the other hand should one spend to preserve the unrecoverable ingredients of life, relationships?

In the school without walls, we don't pay to learn these life lessons. We observe, listen and do. Nature is the main teacher in the school without walls. Nature teaches that when there is hope, people live. Plants, animals and other resources are there for us to learn from and live better (and this is not worshipping them). When we see that with a little amount of force a wet piece of wood can bend while a dry one breaks, we are in school, learning when to bestow lasting values to young people. When we observe a herd of cattle without a leader being the last to arrive at the watering source and consequently drinking dirty water, we are in school, learning the importance of quality leadership. We may witness an old man forced by circumstances to go back to grazing his cattle. We find out what happened to him to cause that and we put our own act together. In short, people are given something to live up to in the school without walls.

The Kamba community of Kenya, East Africa put all lessons or observations into a form which was very basic, memorable, inclusive and non-threatening. In this form, people were talked with. The speaker and listener were both actively involved in the intended message. And most importantly, life's realities were the "props." Think about this: a father tells his high school son to whistle and smile at the same time just to explain that schooling and dating are incompatible. This lesson is encompassed in the saying, "You can't whistle and smile at the same time."

We can call this form of lessons sayings, statements, abstract speech or proverbs. They all are great. They are the palm oil with which words are swallowed. The meaning was never explained. Such unexplained content was used to spark the listener's imagination, understanding and implementation (where appropriate) of the intended purpose of the proverb. Any one of the Kamba proverbs or sayings has more than one implication, thus lending itself to multi-interpretations and sometimes contradictory interpretations. And so is the nature of life.

Traditionally, proverbs were passed on from one generation to another, sometimes without modifications. However, there could be minimum variation on usage which might depict changing times, places or a way of life.

I noted in my previous book, *"Wasya wa Mukamba (The Voice of Mukamba): African Motivational Folktales for All Ages*, that "External influences, mainly western education, religion, and work orientations, have significantly impacted the Kamba way of life. Fathers left their homes to work for property taxes, something whose origin and use were unknown to them. Children were put in schools. Members of the community were introduced to new ways of worship with a particular day devoted to religion."

As these factors were changing the environment in which folktales were usually shared, that is, while members of a family were working together, or warming themselves with the heat of burning acacia branches, or just passing time, the use of proverbs became increasingly rare.

I consider myself very fortunate because my parents and grandfather kept using proverbs and abstract speech to pass on information to us. I have taken the liberty of translating them into English. In some cases, I give some brief description to increase the reader's understanding. English and Kamba languages are far apart and the translation done in this book suffices the intended purpose.

Remember that proverbs or sayings were not interpreted FOR the listeners. Like parables in the Bible, proverbs were to be interpreted BY the listeners. The interpretation following each proverb is the author's perspective and you, the reader, should have your own point of view. You may not agree with all the interpretations, and I believe from your own life journey, you may have many more. These proverbs have had a profound impact on my life that I cannot deny. I can tell a story of nearly every situation when I was told a proverb or when I applied one in a particular situation. The sayings of my parents, grandfather, and a very crucial one from my wife, have been my road map for life.

I have presented the story behind my dad's words, **"that is where men and women get knives to cut their portion of the national cake"** to indicate the impact of abstract communication and to show the unlimited power people can have when they have SOMETHING TO LIVE UP TO and also by knowing that somebody else believes in them. Whether at an early or old age, there are those moments when we all need others to believe in us so that we can believe in our own capabilities. These words by dad were inclusive, non-threatening and he talked with us.

The following is a brief guide for those willing to read the proverbs in Kikamba:

<u>Kamba vowel sounds:</u> A E Ĩ Ị O Ũ U. When reading Kikamba words, A is pronounced as ä (as in father), E as A, Ĩ as in fine, Ị as E, O is still O, Ũ as ü in youth, and U as in flu or blue.

<u>Kamba alphabet:</u> A B D E G H I K L M N O S T U V W Y Z. Not included: C F J P Q R and X. Alphabet letters are harder to substitute and substitution changes the traditional sound of a word.

<u>Naming system:</u>

Akamba — the whole community.

Mũkamba —one person of the community.

Ũkambanĩ — the place where Kamba people live.

Kĩkamba — the language of Kamba people.

The Kamba community (Kambaland) consists of two sub-communities just East of Nairobi. One sub-community has lived in what is known today as the Kĩtwii district, and the other has lived in the Masaku district.

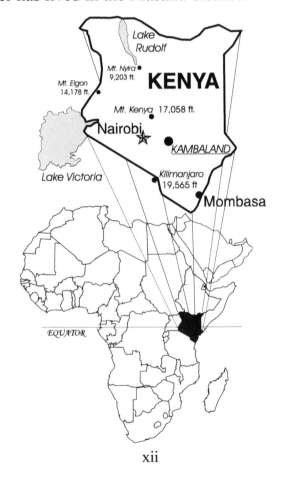

# "My children, that is where men and women get knives to cut their portion of the national cake."

These were my dad's own words in January 1975.

My dad did not have a western education, yet he did anything he could to educate his children. He rewarded us with well-fulfilled promises or encouraged us to try by proper spanking if we performed poorly. In December 1972, I took my grades home after the official closing of school. I had placed sixth in a class of 120 pupils. To my dad that was bad and unacceptable. Only one or two students from Kangundo Primary School would be admitted into government-aided schools after sitting for the seventh-grade examination. So number six was probably bad. I was spanked and denied breakfast. Too bad? No, that was the wake-up call I needed. I had wasted three years of schooling. In each one of these three years, the teacher or my dad, and mostly both, would say my academic performance was not good enough. Thus, I was referred back. This meant spending two years in the same grade. After that spanking in 1972, my dad never spanked me again and I was never referred back again. In fact, my father was able to pride himself on my flying colors and those of my young brother, Major Paul Muyanga Wa Kituku (who was always an academic giant). We both did well and passed the Certificate of Primary Education examination in 1974.

In January 1975, my brother and I were accepted to good schools along with about ten or so other students from our school. My brother was to join Machakos Boys School and I would be attending Tala High School. Great! My dad took us to Nairobi for special shopping. For the first time in our lives we were to purchase and start wearing shoes and long trousers. My father thought that if we had these

Kītukū wa Mūsoo and Kasiva: My Father and Mother in 1975.

"luxurious outfits" before joining high school, they would have interfered with our studies. But now we were ready.

Going to Nairobi was a treat in itself. That trip in 1975 was my third time to go there and my brother's first time. After arriving, before any shopping was done, Dad took us to the main gate of the University of Nairobi. He showed us the University of Nairobi and then said, **"My children, that is where men and**

**women get knives to cut their portion of the national cake."**

I cannot overemphasize the power of this statement. It became the academic road map, for my brother and me. Over twenty years later, I hear it always and in my mind I visit the same place every time I think of it. I feel the same emotional attachment to my father, to my brother and to the universe.

One lesson I have learned since that time is, GIVE ANYONE SOMETHING TO LIVE UP TO (NOT DOWN TO) AND THE SKIES WON'T BE THEIR LIMIT. My father's words cannot and could never be substituted with any one of or even the sum of the many, "How to succeed" books or graduate school programs.

This is why. In high school, we set goals and promised our dad that we too would work hard and go,"... where men and women get knives to cut their portion of the national cake." We both hit the books. After four years of ordinary-level high school, both my brother and I passed with Division I (the equivalent of an A average). We both were chosen to join national schools for Advanced Level High School programs. My brother went to Mangu High School and studied Maths, Physics, Chemistry and Further Maths (tough stuff only done by a few strictly selected students). I went to Shimo La Tewa and studied Physics, Chemistry, Biology and Subsidiary Maths.

To get a clear picture of how tough this was, know that of the 120 students we were together with in primary school, only three, Richard Maithya, my brother and I, made it to this level. My brother and I constantly remembered, "... where men and women get knives to cut their portion of the national cake."

Two years later we sat for the university entrance exam. This was known to be an exterminator. For every 100 students, less than ten made it to university. Again, we both made it, an unheard of incident where two brothers pass that exam at the same time. We were actually able to go "... where men and women get knives to cut their portion of the national cake." Besides my brother and me, none of the 120 other primary school classmates made it to university.

I have known that there is a global cake where each individual needs his or her own portion. Education is the only knife which each one can use to get his or her share.

Parents and teachers, are we showing young people where men and women get knives to cut their portion of the global cake? What kind of knives are they getting? And how are they getting them?

The world is changing rapidly, and it will never be the same again. Isolation will never be the way to live. With the rate of technological development, advanced information systems and the opening of international borders, our children will be forced to compete for the jobs in their own hometown with others from foreign lands.

Let's commit to showing them, "... where men and women get knives to cut their portion of the global cake."

Vincent Kituku

January 1997

"Mbaa ngeeka meethĩiwe mataneka."

**P**rocrastinators are caught by events before they do anything.

Those who keep saying, "I will do this or that whenever" mostly end up doing nothing.

"Syalisya ĩtina inyusyaa mũuluũ."

# When they (cattle) stay behind, they drink dirty water.

When a herd of cattle happens to be the last one to arrive at the water source, it ends up drinking water which has already been made dirty by others. When someone takes the "back seat" of life, he/she most likely will settle for "leftovers" if there are any.

"Mūndū ūteyĩuna ndauna ũngĩ."

**H**e/she who cannot benefit himself/herself cannot benefit another person.

Somebody who cannot work and support himself/herself cannot expect to benefit others. This was used during courtship when a boy's activeness was an indicator that he was capable of supporting his wife and children. My mother tells me that she was told (by her grandmother) to make sure that her husband was somebody with a great appetite for food. This would ensure that he worked hard to satisfy his appetite and thus hers.

"Mūkamba akolow'a too ni kīthuma kya
ng'ombe yake."

A Mukamba sleeps well only when
he lies on the hide of his own cow.

Cows could be raided from other
neighboring communities or could be gifts
from relatives. However, lying on the hide of
an animal one had not raised was not
considered a noble experience. Thus, the
implication of this saying is that one is only
happy when he/she is not depending on others
for his/her livelihood.

"Malĩ ndĩetwe nĩ kwĩtwa."

**W**ealth cannot be told to come. One has to work for it or inherit it from others.

"Ũla ũkũnyeewa nĩwe wĩthũaa."

# He/she whose body is itching, scratches himself/herself.

Don't wait for others to formulate your success path. It's your life, family, career and soul; you are responsible for your life.

"Kana kanini kathamba moko nĩkaĩsyaa na asumbĩ."

# A child who washes his/her hands eats with kings.

Age is not what determines one's social status.  Character does.

"Ngitĩ nĩyo yĩtusaa mwanga."

# A dog makes itself unworthy of respect.

Pets relate differently to people of diverse backgrounds. For example, in my culture, dogs are for protecting the owner and his/her property. Dogs mostly hunt their own food and sometimes food for the owner. Occasionally, a dog would start eating chickens, stealing and eating eggs or eating people's food without their consent. These acts led to the dog being less respected and not trusted. This saying may be used to indicate that one's character determines the respect he/she gets especially if there are no existing stereotypes.

"Kũtũ kũla kwĩwaa ngania nũnakwie
kwĩwĩkaa nĩ kũngĩ."

The ear which hears "so and so passed away" is heard of by another one.

This is a reminder that all exit from this world the same way. As such, let's be kind to one another.

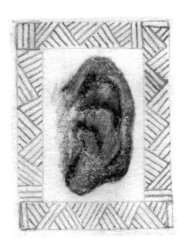

"Kĩla mũndũ ewonzu wake."

# Everybody has his/her own weakness.

This is to say that while we are pointing at the weakness of others, we should know that we have our own. When you point at someone with one finger, it's good to know that your other three (less the thumb) fingers of the pointing hand, are pointing at you.

"Mũeni nĩ kĩw'ũ kĩvĩtĩte."

# A visitor is like passing water.

Since the visitor is not going to live with you forever, treat him/her well.

"Ũla wĩ kĩvetanĩ ndũthekaa ũla wĩ iko."

# The firewood next to the fireplace cannot mock the burning wood.

In life, one should not rejoice in the downfall of others.

"Mũsyai ndathekaa ũla ũngĩ."

# A parent cannot mock another parent.

This is used in reference to the behavior of one parent's child or children. If the character of the children of a particular parent leaves a lot to be desired, other parents should not rejoice.

## "Ĩthyoma yĩmwe yĩitwa mwana mwĩkũyũ."

**A**child cannot become a Kikuyu just because of one mispronunciation.

Kamba and Kikuyu dialects are very close. People from either group occasionally pronounce some words like those of the other group. This saying indicates no one should be classified wrongly based on perception or be given group identity based on one characteristic.

"Mbũi nzaũ yaa yenewe."

# A white goat gets lost while it's still being watched.

This saying was used as a warning showing that one could easily lose his/her good characteristics without being noticed by others. As such, one has to watch what he/she does carefully. Those responsible for the youth were also to put forth extra effort "just in-case."

"Kĩla kĩtũngaa mũtumĩa ndĩthya
ndethĩawa akĩsĩ."

# An old man never knows what causes him to watch cattle at his old age.

In the Kamba Community, the grazing of family cattle was the responsibility of young boys. In some situations, another person took care of the cattle if a boy was not available. This saying was used to warn people of lifestyles which could lead them to undergo a dreaded experience for the second time.

"Kĩkondu akengie kĩtũla masyaĩe nzĩanĩ,
kĩtũla alĩka athela."

**A**solanum      plant      (inedible)
convinced    an    edible    berry
**bearing plant that they both bear
fruits beside a trail. The edible plant
ended up having all its fruits eaten
completely.**

This saying challenges people to
understand the background of their role models
or peers before trying to live like them.
Sometimes, people watch actors and imitate
whatever behavior the actors portray. The
imitated behavior may harm the imitator's life
while the actor is not negatively affected.

17

"Weew'a yĩla ĩvĩsĩ kana yĩlĩtu ya ngania manya nĩ meka mayo."

**W**hen you hear about the son or daughter of so and so, know it's because of his/her (son's or daughter's) actions.

One is judged based on his/her individual actions. This saying encourages people to earn their own respect in a community, but not to depend on their parents' name, good or bad.

"Vala ya mbee ya kinya novo ya kelĩ
ĩkinyaa."

# Where the first one steps is where the second one steps.

When a cow is walking, the left hind leg lands on or near the spot where the left front leg had landed. This saying is used to show that children pattern their lifestyle after that of their parents or other adults who deal with them (children) as they grow. It warns adults to watch what they do, or say. A child is just about to "step in" on his/her (adult) life pattern. This reminds me of a note I got when our son Kĩthetheesyo was born. It talked about the "little eyes" which are "always upon you."

"Ngi ĩmwe yoasya ĩsama."

# One fly causes a chunk of meat to be rotten.

One "bad apple" can have major impact in a system.

"Kĩthiia kyumanasya nthĩ na mĩw'a."

# An acacia tree comes forth from the ground with thorns.

Character and civility are built when one is young.

"Kana nĩ yumba yĩũ."

# A child is like wet clay.

It is easy to mold wet clay to any shape or object. A child easily follows what he/she hears or sees.

"Vai ũtinda na mũkũndũ ndakũndũke."

No one stays with somebody who has chicken pox, without getting it (unless he/she had it before or is vaccinated against it).

One is socially influenced by those with whom he/she associates.

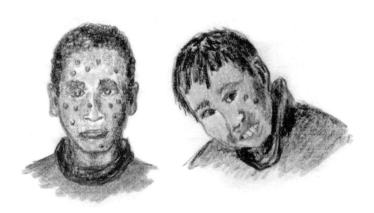

"Vai nzaũ yanasya ĩsyũkonĩ mĩaka yoonthe."

There is no one bull which can be the greatest fighter in a ridge every year.

In any given time, there was always one bull that dominated a whole herd. But with time, another bull would rise and overpower the aging one. The lesson from this observation is live and let others live. Appreciate others knowing that today they may need you, while you may need them tomorrow.

"Ndamanya ndĩtogoesya."

# If I knew... is never known ahead of time.

Used when an unexpected situation or experience arose.

"Kwoonekie kwa kuma kwa kũthi
kũyaa."

## Since there was a place to leave, a place to go can be found.

Moving from one place to another was a common practice. As such, a change was not a threat. Or viewed from another perspective, if one survives an experience, chances are that he/she will thrive in another one of the same nature.

"Kaatemwa nĩ lũĩ nĩko koĩ "

**A chick that has been attacked by a hawk knows the impact of the experience.**

Experience is the best teacher (although it may not be the most effective teacher always).

"Nzaũ ngũũ yũkitaa na kĩleelo."

An old steer fights with a definite strategy.

Experience is the best tool.

"Mũtinda weka asyaa nyinyia nowe mũui."

# The one who stays alone thinks his mother is the only one who cooks.

Because of the community orientation of the Kamba people, it was rare to see a loner. This means if one gets beyond his/her comfort zone, he/she learns new things and experiences.

"Nyūmba ya ndulũ noĩkathi na ngalĩ."

# The house of Ndulu will one day drive.

My close friends and I coined this saying when we were at Tala High School. We walked to school. Some walked six miles one way. To drive was a dream, but we consoled ourselves by working on our hope that if we did our homework, we would drive one day. Why we called ourselves the house of Ndulu; I have no clear memory, but it could depict our state of limited resources while again presenting the positive impact of having something to live up to. We were about 10. Seven of us have driven since then. In America this is not big deal. It is, however, in an area where only less than 10% of the country's population drives.

## "Mũnyu wa ngai nduĩawa."

# The salt of God is not rained upon.

Salt in a natural environment, when rained upon, melts and loses its usefulness. It can't be used to make food tasty. This saying, however, presents the fact that God's goodness is not seasonal. Neither is it negatively affected by other forces. At times, we may be experiencing storms (sickness, grief, rocky relationships, spiritual darkness, job insecurity) that are so strong the future seems unbearable. Remember the salt of God is not rained upon. Those storms will come to pass and leave God's goodness (love for us) still intact. Even during the storms, He is there to lift us above the storms, lest the rain fall upon His salt.

"Syathĩ na mavinda ni sya ngai."

# Plans and seasons are under the mercy of God.

People make plans and stipulate the time to accomplish them. In the end, the plans and timing depend on God. This is an area in which we need to pray. Today we frequently hear, "I can create my own success." What is the will of God in your plans and timing? Is He in your plans and timing? He controls the human breath. Plan and make a schedule; then say by the grace of God you hope to accomplish your goals.

"Thĩna ndũaa ũkĩtaa kũnyamasya."

# **P**overty never kills; it's just a bother.

There is hope. Keep holding on and act positively.

"Kava kũthaũka na malĩ kũte kũthaũka
na mweene."

It's better to interfere with a
person's wealth than to interfere
with the person.

Wealth can be gained, lost and
regained. People are not regained.

"Mūtũi atumaa ndoo ĩinyunga."

# A neighbor repairs a smelling pile.

A neighbor helps at critical moments and as such needs to be appreciated.

"Vala nthũ yĩkaw'a tivo ĩvalũkaa."

# Where an enemy is thrown, is not where he/she falls.

This was a warning against evil acts toward one's real or perceived enemies. While the wish would be for the enemy to experience the worst in life, nature has its way of accepting and rewarding the enemy.

"Iīma nosyo itakomanaa."

# Hills never meet.

People do. This saying is used mostly when people are affirming that they will meet again, or when one is being warned not to stay aloof.

"Vai usya mũũi na akatheka."

# No one can whistle and smile at the same time.

It's impossible to achieve anything when one engages in two incompatible goals. My father told me this wonderful saying when I was in high school. He wanted me to concentrate on school and not to overindulge with dating activities. He asked me to whistle and then smile. I did. Then he asked me to do both at once. I couldn't.

"Mũsyĩ wa ũtukũ ũtũngĩlawa vala wesĩla."

A night's arrow is sent back in the same direction from which it comes.

This reminds people to appreciate those who have helped them.

"Mbũi ya mana ndĩ syaawa maeo."

**A free goat is never checked whether it has teeth.**

Appreciate what you get free irrespective of its condition. This is similar to saying, "Don't look a gift horse in the mouth."

"Kĩsomo nĩ ĩkũmbĩ yĩte ngulu."

# Education is a barn with no weevils.

Knowledge is like a barn which has no seed-eating organisms. When you have it, it's yours to retrieve and use as needed. You can also add to the barn. My dad used to tell us that our education is probably the only thing for which nobody else can claim co-ownership.

"Kīw'ū kīnetīka kīikolanaw'a."

# Spilled water cannot be collected.

There is no need to waste time and energy on bygones. No one has control of the past. You can only learn from it and move to the future.

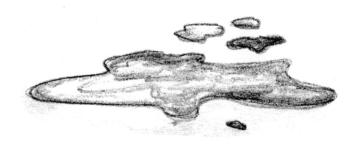

"Makwata nde kĩndũ."

# He who holds on to everything has nothing.

Trying to be everything, everywhere, all the time leads one to achieve nothing. To succeed at one's life goals, one has to focus and engage in compatible projects.

"Syaasya ndongoi inyusyaa mũuluũ."

# When they (cattle) lack a leader, they drink dirty water.

In every herd of cattle, one, usually the oldest, knew all the paths to grazing and watering sources. This cow, bull or steer, was the herd's leader. When a herd lacked a leader, chances were that it would be the last one to arrive at the water source, and end up drinking water which had already been made dirty by other herds. Today we can associate most social downfalls to the lack of true leaders in all aspects of life, lack of positive role models at home, church, work-place or school. This conspicuous absence of "human leaders" probably explains why societies are drinking social "dirty water," and why there is an increase of family breakdown, crime, teen pregnancy, school dropouts, unmotivated workers, destruction of natural resources, and spiritual emptiness.

"Thome wĩ ngũĩ waĩaa ĩkoma ya mũtumĩa."

An old man's tobacco container may get lost around his fireplace (home) if there is no respect.

In the Kamba community, men stayed away from the cooking place. There was a fireplace (located in a place where they could see the whole homestead) where they visited with other men and counseled the young boys. Creative order which encouraged a relaxed, yet respectful atmosphere, was necessary to accomplish any progress. This saying may also indicate the necessity for respect and strong leadership.

"Wĩĩthya mang'ula kũla tũnaĩthisye."

# You are grazing where we have already grazed.

Young people somehow have the impression that their parents have no idea on their (youth) life experiences. This saying affirms that whatever the youth is experiencing or doing is not new or strange. This is a traditional saying, but today I guess there are some "strange" things happening.

"Ndaĩa ĩkĩtaa kwĩmanthĩwa."

# Respect is earned by an individual.

"Mbũi yĩ mwana ndyũaawa."

# A goat with a kid is not eaten.

This calls for respect and honor to parents. From another perspective, it may mean that the main source of support should not be tampered with.

## "Ũtatia, ndethĩa."

# He who can't let go, can't find.

This is for encouraging people to let go of expectations, experiences or projects that are not beneficial; and to have time to find new opportunities. Letting go is especially useful in our times because there is no job security. Thus we may need to let go of some of the typical expectations we may have for long-term employment.

"Walea ũkonzwa wĩmwĩé, wooma ndũkonzeka."

If it's not straightened when its still wet, it's impossible to straighten it when it's dry.

When one has to straighten a piece of wood, it's only possible when the wood is wet. When the wood is dry, it breaks if force is used to straighten it. In life there is an appropriate time for everything. Time to foster values, teach and train to serve, time to adjust and meet demands of change. When that opportunity is missed, there may never be another chance. This saying was used mostly to emphasize the need for fostering positive life qualities in youth when there was still hope (still flexible).

"Mūndū mūe nde nguma ūtūinī."

# A witch doctor has no honor in his/her own village.

Those who live with you rarely recognize your credentials. Similar to saying an expert has to come from at least 50 miles away from town.

"Kyūma kĩkũnawa kĩkĩvyũ."

**A** metal is hit (to make the needed shape) when it's hot.

An opportunity is seized when it's appropriate. Values are fostered when there is hope.

"Kalula katune katunĭvaw'a nĩ
kũnengeleanĩlw'a."

# A calabash is made red by being passed on.

This saying is based on a traditional beer drinking practice of the Kamba people. When men sat to drink beer, one of them would pour the beer from a gourd into a calabash. He would then take a sip and pass it on to the next one, who in turn, would take a sip before passing it on. The calabash's normal cream color turned reddish as a result of the oil from the different hands.

Reddish color symbolizes beauty. The more a calabash was passed on, the faster it became red. The more we share our experiences, talents, gifts, and hopes, the more beautiful life becomes.

"Ndanyuka mbola nĩyĩsyaa kũmelya."

# An animal that chews slowly still swallows.

Pursue your goals even if they take a long time. If you continuously work on them, you will accomplish them. Don't worry about what you don't have. Begin with what you have, and work on them bit by bit. Ted Gibson, a friend of mine, told me that his father used to say, "nothing will ever be attempted if all obstacles must be removed first." Just start and chew slowly, you will eventually swallow.

"Vai kĩasa kĩte mũthya."

# There is no journey without an end.

Hold on to your "journey." There will be an end. Journey indicates projects or long-awaited expectations.

"Mbee ndĩ ũmũĩ."

# No one knows the future or what is ahead.

As such, hope for the best but prepare for uncertainties.

"Kĩtaee nĩkyũkaa."

# Expectations do fail.

Prepare for uncertainties.

"Mwana ũla mũkũũ eanene na ĩthe."

# The first-born, is like a father.

This is a major Kamba perspective which bestows family responsibilities on the first son, especially in the absence of the father.

"Mwĩsũkũũe wa mũndũ nĩ ngovia ya
ũsumbĩ."

# The grandchild of a person is his/her crown.

A grandchild is a crown. Enjoy it and respond to the responsibilities that pertain to it.

"Mũnoi tiwe mũi."

# The laborer is not the benefactor.

This presents the situation where one labors and a different person benefits from his/her sweat. This is so because of the Kamba family structure. Those blessed with earthly possessions provide for the well-being of needy family or community members.

"Nzou ndĩemawa nĩ mũwongo wayo."

# An elephant is never defeated in carrying its own tusks.

This reflects the fact that parents should be responsible for their own children. Or one should be responsible for his\her own livelihood.

"Ndũkaaumange sua yĩtanathũa."

# **Don't curse the sun before sunset.**

Don't give up on life before you die. Don't give up on any project before you get its benefits or understand why it can't work (keep learning).

"Vai mbua ĩtakya."

# There is no rainfall that never ends.

There is no experience or project with endless benefits. Think beyond your current productivity level, skills, knowledge, spiritual level, and family ties. Then develop strategies for doing even better in the long run.

"Vai kĩĩma kĩsinda ĩny'ũũ nzeve."

# There is no hill with more air than the nose.

Any hill has enough air to support the lives on it just as the nose has enough air to support the body system it's supposed to. What matters is the fact that both are efficient. It doesn't matter whether you are a hill or nose, you'd better be efficient in your life goals. This does not mean you can't make mistakes. Be efficient in recognizing and learning from your mistakes. Use your potential and do your best. It doesn't pay to compare yourself with others.

"Mũndũ ekĩawa wathe nĩkĩndũ ũvikya."

# Somebody is made weak/sick by an object he/she can carry.

Lifting things is a common practice. If an object is too heavy, no one carries it. However, over and over again people carry the light objects that eventually affect the health of the carrier. This indicates that people are affected by the habits they are used to.

"Kĩkuu kĩĩtina nĩkyo kĩĩtw'ĩkanasya."

# A gourd with a relatively flat bottom sits on its own.

Gourds have either a rounded or a relatively flat bottom. A gourd with a rounded bottom requires support to stay upright. Most of the time a hole is dug in the ground into which the circular bottom fits well, thus the gourd stays upright. A gourd with a flat bottom needs no support.

A person with knowledge, skills, ability, integrity, and reputation can survive and thrive on his/her own.

## "Vai mbua ĩte ũmuu."

# There is no rainfall that never brings mosquitoes.

There is no beneficial experience or project in life that does not have side effects (time away from family, borrowing money to start business, spending time in school).

"Mbaa kwona meanene na mbaa
kwaĩwa."

# Those who have and those who don't, are equal.

Equality in life should be independent of possessions. Or those who have possessions can lose them and those who don't can gain them.

"Nĩ syumaa ũkavi na ikethĩa ene."

# They (cattle) may be brought from Maasailand only to be owned by others.

Before the coming of the British to Kenya, the Kamba and Maasai people would raid cattle from each other. The raided cattle were distributed among all members of the raiding Kamba village, those who raided and those who stayed home. This saying shows that the raider was not necessarily the final owner.

"Ũseo ndũetwe nĩ kwĩtwa."

# Success can't be achieved by only talking about it.

For one to succeed, he/she has to act and be successful. Sitting and wishing can never bring success.

"Ndũkakĩe syũki ũtene mwaki."

# Don't be afraid of smoke before you see the fire.

Don't be afraid to move on with your goals just because of the limitations you can identify outright. Winners are not scared by the smoke. Losers are kept off by it.

"Nĩ syaawa ĩtina na ĩ kang'oania mbia."

# A bull can be young and yet lock horns with the old ones.

Age should not deter one from achieving life dreams.

"Mbua ya ĩmantha ti ĩmwe."

# There is more than one season for planting.

People are reminded that in life, one has more than one chance to search for his/her opportunities, especially after a failure. You can still succeed.

"Mavundi maingĩ maanangie nyũmba
ya ngavana."

# M any mansions destroyed the governor's house.

The governor was a colonial leader and had the highest administrative office in the country. This saying indicates that many opinions do not necessarily bring forth a great product. To succeed, you have to re-evaluate and select other people's opinions carefully.

"Kasaũ kakya nĩko kenyenyaa
mũongo."

# An orphan calf licks its own back.

The fact that you have no one to hold your hand in life does not mean you can't succeed.

"Kĩndũ kĩnene kĩthũku no kĩtau."

# The only thing that is bad when it's big is a wound.

In most cases big size was associated with success. Large tracts of land, gourds, pots, houses, families, herds of cattle and other goods all depicted success. A wound when big was a problem.

"Kyaa Kĩmwe kĩyũaa ndaa."

# One finger cannot kill a louse.

This saying calls for unity or team spirit when undertaking any project. A louse, though small, was killed by pressing it with the two thumb nails.

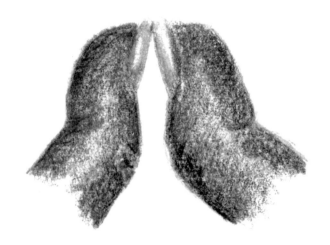

"Yenda mũno ĩtusaa mũkautĩ."

# When it (a cow) 'over loves', it cuts the umbilical cord.

Implies that when a cow keeps on licking the umbilical cord of its newborn calf, the cord may get cut near the stomach, thus, opening an entrance for bacteria that may eventually cause death. This is a warning given to parents not to neglect traditional disciplining (this is not child abuse, it's done for somebody you love and wish him/her the best in life) and training of children.

"Malĩ nĩyonawa na mũndũ ndoneka."

# Wealth can be found but not people.

The greatest resource anyone can have in any undertaking is people. Value them. They are more valuable than wealth.

"Vandũ ndatia kaũ nditia maya."

# Wherever I can't leave a fight, I shouldn't leave a feast.

This is another saying my friends and I coined (although I am not positive it hasn't been used elsewhere) when we where at Tala High School. When one was offered something to eat by other students, he accepted it and used this saying to show that his relationship with his host was for better or worse.

"Ĩnyũũ yalea kanyua ndũya."

# What the nose has refused, the mouth can't eat.

Serious stuff. What one parent says no to, the other one should not go against it (at least not in the presence of the children or in public).

"Mūndū ūmwe ndetwa mbaa ngania."

# An individual can't be referred to as the family of so and so.

This emphasizes the value placed on families. And remember, love makes a family.

"Ũkethaa kĩla wavanda."

**Y**ou reap what you sow.

"Wenda ũmanya nyamũ nthũku kiita
ĩswii yayo."

# If you want to know whether an animal is fierce, touch its baby.

This warning is for those who would try
to be mean to young children.  Their parents
and other relatives fight for them.

# *Other Memorable Statements*

## From my parents, Kituku and Kasiva:

"Son, before you buy a car or build a house, make sure your family is well fed and clothed. Always buy enough food to last more than a day. When your family is satisfied with those two things, then invest in anything else."

"Son, always strive to build a strong home before constructing a house."

"Friends are like clothes; not all sizes fit you."

They always wanted us, their children, to have friends who were involved with school, church, and the community.

"Be considerate of needy folks; you never know when you are entertaining an angel."

"The light you shine in the lives of others illuminates your own life. Let your light shine brightly."

"The bread you earn with your sweat satisfies more and longer than the bread passed on to you."

"When a man and a woman get married, each has a sample of light he/she brings into the marriage. At times, one light may be off. It is the responsibility of the one whose light is still on, to hold it high for the sake of the children, and also to provide light when the other spouse wants his/her lamp re-lighted."

## From my grandfather, Musoo:

"The great and life-lasting school has no walls." He used to tell me nature was my school.

"There is no man who has ever been scolded by his wife as long as he comes home from hunting with his bows, arrows, and meat."

"If there was no meat, the wife would say, 'Children, sit down. Don't stand up unless you want your eyes to get poked with these bows and arrows that never kill anything.'"

"If there was meat, the wife would say, 'Children, don't sit down. Don't you see your father needs help with his bows and arrows plus the meat?'"

This was to encourage his grandchildren to always strive to bring home the fruits of their sweat. Even in this modern day, families appreciate if they can see the benefits of the time their spouse has taken away from the family.

"Son, you can lose your health and sometimes regain it; wealth can be regained after losing it; you can lose many things in life and regain them. Family times and trust may never be regained."

## From my grandmother, Mbinya:

"My child, what I give you is more valuable than what wealth can give you. Have my blessings." She was very poor and she always blessed me when we met on my way to Tala High School. The ritual of blessing one's relatives has had a positive influence on the Kamba people. Because of the blessings, those who have been blessed always have hope to do better in life. Many even change their lifestyle for better following the blessing ritual. It is very important that parents bless their children. It's an act of good will. A blessed individual could prosper materially, but the most important aspect is living a peaceful life.

## From my wife, Theresia Wanza Muli :

"Honey, don't try to be faithful to me in our marriage. Just work hard and be honest with yourself, and faithful to God. That will be enough for me."

Dr. Kituku presents seminars, workshops, and keynote speeches customized to your group needs. Here is a sample of the topics that are covered.

## COMPLETE SUCCESS PACKAGE:

**Dynamics of Work Life**
*(Buffaloes In Our Lives)*

**Visionary Journey**
*(Beyond the Lion)*

**What Matters in Times of Change**
*(The Jungle Rod: Master of Change)*

**The Light that Illuminates Your Paths**
*(Hold It For Me So That I Can Make The Bed)*

**Re-Focusing Your Life After Change**
*(Are Your Buffaloes at Large?)*

**Multi-Cultural Crucible**
*(Inside-out; Diversity)*

Special Workshops Offered by Dr. Kituku through Boise State University:

**Introduction to Swahili**

**African Folk Tales**

**African Literature**

**Culture and Conservation of African Wildlife**

**The Art of Storytelling**

## Audio Cassette Materials

**Enjoy listening to *The Voice of Mukamba* on a quality audio cassette.** Studio recording by Dr. Kituku contains the following folktales: The Hampster's Piece of a Tail, Monkey and the Shark, A Cow and a Frog's Family, Hyena and the Rock, Mūtei and a Tiger, The Greedy Dog, Matema and Mūmanyi, Hare and Hyena, Wasp and Fly, Chameleon and Raven, A Monkey is a Monkey, An Old Man and a Boy, A Chicken and a Shilling, Ndothya and Hyena, Hunting on the Plains, Masūnga and Kaindi, and The Water Banana.

**The Voice Of Mukamba: East African Folktales told by Dr. Kituku      $9.50**

Other Cassettes Recorded by Dr. Kituku:

**Buffaloes in the Workplace: Surviving and Thriving Workplace Change as a Jungle Rod!      $9.50**

**The Light That Illuminates Your Path: (Hold It For Me So That I Can Make The Bed)      $9.50**

***To Order*** Tape Sets or Additional Copies of this book please send $9.50 (in Idaho add 5% sales tax) plus $1.50 shipping and handling for each item to the address below.

**For information about workshops, seminars and keynote speeches contact:**

> **Dr. Vincent Kituku**
> **PO Box 7152**
> **Boise, Idaho 83707**
> **Phone (208) 939-7216**

**Another Book by Dr. Kituku:**

*East African Folktales For All Ages: from The Voice Of Mukamba*, Published by August House, 1997. Available at your local bookstore.